ALL THE TIME

YOU WANT

ALL THE TIME YOU WANT

SELECTED POEMS
1977 – 2017

Keith Taylor

DZANC
BOOKS

DZANC
BOOKS

2580 Craig Rd.
Ann Arbor, MI 48103
www.dzancbooks.org

First Edition: January 2024
Cover design by Shoshana Schultz
Cover painting by Khaled Al Saa'i, used with the permission of the University of Michigan Museum of Art
Interior design by Michelle Dotter

ISBN: 9781950539901

Printed in the United States of America

10   9   8   7   6   5   4   3   2   1

for Christine

companion
through all these poems

A NOTE TO THE READER

THESE POEMS ARE ARRANGED in roughly chronological order, or as close to that as I've been able to remember. That order is based on the time of their first composition, on the time when I was working on them most intensely, not on their first publication. Some were extensively revised much later and appeared in journals, in books, or in chapbooks even decades after I began working on them. The versions selected here are the most recent incarnations.

ALL THE TIME

YOU WANT

THE HOLY DANCE

We hear they've opened
an old folks home
in her name. We're proud.

We remember her black dresses
shining like bibles, her hand
moving lightly over our backs and arms,

her prayers, long and touching
(I timed her once—
sixteen minutes of grace before supper).

Only an old man
who moved south, to Nebraska,
remembers how she moved

and the hard burning
behind her
at the barn dance

where she turned,
fast,
spinning,

her white dress swirling out,
quicker, until everything
pulled in, even light.

FIRST DANCE

Black-haired Doreen—
the only girl with glasses in our class,
the only Catholic I knew,
the first child I ever saw dance.
We had heard that Catholics
danced, but when we snuck up
to their clapboard church at the edge
of town and saw the Virgin
through the window, we ran away—so young
we still believed all idols were devils.
We told brave stories about women
in long black dresses dancing around
a golden statue.
     But when Doreen
danced at show-and-tell, when
those tiny black shoes clicked
so fast against the hardwood floor,
I almost cried. I wanted to dance.
It did not feel like sin.

FOR MARILYN AND THE ROOT CELLAR

She was a year older
and knew things
so I had followed her

here, deep into the center
of the only hill
in our prairie lives.

I held the light, slightly shaking,
while she brushed the shavings aside
and unearthed two potatoes

buried below roots
for warmth, still slowly growing
in memory of summer.

She cut the nubs away,
peeled back the skin
to potato whiteness,

and here, in the one place
we were told never to visit,
we shared the raw food
we were told never to touch.

THE HOUSEPAINTER'S RECREATION

The housepainter goes to bars
where interested women ask
him what he does. He says—
I paint. They treat him
with respect, even awe; they see
brown paint under his nails
and imagine he paints dark
canvases, full of angst
and sorrow. He smiles
sadly when they talk to him.
One offers to pose, but he says—
I don't do people. She understands.

REFUSING PYGMALION

Perhaps that legend
of a man loving
perfectly sculpted stone
is right. Perhaps
we do create
everything we love. But I
haven't carved this
woman from white marble,
haven't fasted, prayed,
sacrificed for a god to make
her live. She is a sudden
gift, beautiful and marred
by a red scar across her back.
She has uneven hips.

SNOWBOUND

On Belle Isle, the hottest day
of the year, Walter,
nine years old, shouted
when wind hit the fountain
and white sprayed over us,

Look! Look!
It's snow!

WHITE PINE STUMPS

Logging slash burned
for months, leaving stumps
as solid as memory
and five feet across.

We find them when we pass
from scrub oak and brambles
to the grass and deep shade
of those places far off the road
where our forest has matured again,
this time in beech
and maple filled with birds
the old loggers never imagined
in their evergreen world.

GUILTY AT THE RAPTURE

All things good would rise
into air, pulled from dirt and sky,
from cars left driverless
below, slamming into trees.

That would be my first clue.
On my ride home from the river—
burning on my gold Schwinn
and sucking hard on a mint to smother
the newspaper cigarette I'd just smoked
in a stand of scrub willow—
I would have to dodge
machines abandoned by vanished Christians,
glorified while driving back from work
after centuries of trial.

I would know a final loneliness
before I screamed through the back door
and found supper smoldering over gas.
My parents gone. Even my sister—
only a hair less guilty—
called to her celestial chorus.
I would be alone in a world
of smokers, crooks, murderers,
of moviegoers, gamblers, and sex fiends,
left, at last, alone in a world
without one hope of grace.

BANSHEE

I've told the story so many times
it has assumed its own truth,
how on Aranmore off Donegal
after I was fired from the hostel
and moved up to the crofter's
shack where the doctor lived,
how we stayed up almost every
night and listened to the wind
blow around us all through November.
How one night while a force nine
blew itself out against Ireland
the island girl who came to clean
every other week stayed
with us to swap stories with Doctor
Collins about heroes and the island
and fishing. We drank port waiting
for one good story to take shape.
How a scream that wasn't wind
or human, certainly not bird
or airplane, went over the shack.
I jerked fast enough to make
my glasses fly off. The doctor,
a man of science and a cynic,
was frightened too. Only the island
girl, who really did have red hair,
looked calm. *The witch of death,*
she said and—then she did it—
she chuckled. An hour later a man
came to tell us in bad English

that a woman who lived by the church
had died and would the doctor come
to sign all the necessary papers.
She was over ninety and never
left the island before her flight
this wild and windy night.

LANDED IMMIGRANTS

No, nothing like your huddled
masses with exotic Old
World diseases. No endless
weeks aboard ship sailing to
a vague Eden. Just a rust
brown '58 Chevrolet
pulling a family of four
and a U-Haul southeast from
Moose Jaw into this foreign
land, on July Fourth. Main Street
in Portal, North Dakota,
was blocked off early; bunting
and flags were already up.
By Fargo the bands were out.
Between floats Indians rode
their nervous Appaloosas,
looked like Indians we knew,
wore the same buckskins, never
looked down, and always ignored
the police, who held us up,
our motor running, until
the Minutemen with their pipes
marched past and "Yankee Doodle"
was lost in a sudden breeze.
Then the car broke down. Steam sprayed
out the grill, even seeped back
through the floorboards. The gears locked.
And Chicago, our future,
seemed an impossible dream,

a new television show
with machine guns and barrels
of illegal whiskey brought
from Canada—Chicago,
where good guys looked bad and where
gangsters finally bought it.

DETROIT DANCING, 1948

In memoriam: Leo Golus

Everyone home from the war with stories
to tell. Except me, of course. Just a bit
too young to know the horrors of Iwo,
Normandy, the Bulge, I spent the duration
peddling popcorn outside a theater on
Gratiot; later, groceries at the Market.
No woman would be wowed by any yarns
I could spin. And I'd never win a turkey
with my looks. You see, everyone needs
an angle. At the Polish National Alliance
in Hamtramck the women gathered dutifully
around their returning heroes, wide-eyed
in the presence of such courage. But when
they danced, they danced alone, their arms
circling the smoke from a hundred cigarettes.
With luck one might find another woman
anxious to show her grace. Think of it,
years spent watching two women, nineteen
or twenty, sway each other over
the stained floor. So I taught myself dancing,
downstairs, at home, in the old neighborhood,
humming "Moonlight Serenade" for rhythm,
waltzing the broom, my partner, from coal bin
to canning jars, learning to finish
with a flourish (dipping its bristled head
gently toward the cement), until I could
walk into any club anywhere in the city,
pick out any woman, turn her once

across the floor, and, if I didn't sweep
her off her feet, I'd hear at least
(and this was almost enough, then)
that I was certainly light on mine.

LIVING HERE

In the middle of the thing
or walking through the arcade, I wait—

I wait because the only lesson
I've learned is that the gift comes

in its own time, and goes
without scent or taste or flashing signs.

WEATHER REPORT

for Khaled Mattawa

You wouldn't believe the green.
It still startles me, so unexpectedly
there, outside the window
where I've learned to look
for winter. Grass, and the tips
of spruce branches, flower stems.
Crocuses have come and gone
already. Hyacinths and tulips
are in full bloom, daffodils
past their peak. Only last
week rain turned to snow
for a night and left a white
dusting on the pile of peat
beside the bed where Christine
is planting new perennials.
It's April. The weather's
flipping from early summer
to late winter and I can't
go two days without shouting
at people I don't know
about things I barely understand.
When the finches came
to our feeder this morning,
I saw they had finished
their molt, and seemed as bright
as your Mediterranean,
your desert sun. Even this
close to the Arctic we can't

go four months without
at least one blossom hidden
somewhere in our backyard.

DETAIL FROM THE GARDEN OF DELIGHTS

There's a way out. In the back
corner under mulberry bushes and a stand
of juniper, we hide with our familiar
spirits. We dance discreetly naked.

We are fed impossible raspberries
by a goldfinch who does all the work
and doesn't mind. We nestle into the down
on his back and drift off into flying sleep.

If occasionally we are filled
with the longing to look down
at new places, our hair turns red
and we ride a robin, windblown
only by the breeze from his wings.

We can see roseate spoonbills
on the backs of ewes, cows with paws.
No houses anywhere. No business.
No church. No school. An endless garden.

We kiss in the shade cast by a kingfisher,
who has come to watch, even though
our streams are buried and we offer
nothing but the spectacle of joy.

WCTU

Lyle Stauffer always won. We memorized long poems about the horrors of drink, about fathers who beat mothers then disappeared for days into smoky taverns, about a brave eight-year-old who wandered streets filled with loose women and drunks until she found Dad and brought him home to the little white house. Father would kneel before mother, cry, and swear to the Highest Authority that it would never happen again.

We practiced our gestures. We learned to break our voices at the moment when the child found father slumped in his barroom chair. She shook the sleeve of his jacket until he looked up and, in his stupor, slapped her face. A drop of blood in the corner of the child's mouth. A faint recognition would come, finally, into father's red eyes. In a blinding moment of repentance, he rose and followed the child out into the pure night air.

We recited our poems for the local chapter of the Women's Christian Temperance Union. Some of us forgot the words and stumbled and had to repeat whole stanzas. We knew the winner would be the one who could make Auntie Edna Eby weep.

Lyle never forgot his words. He could make Auntie Edna sob out loud. He always got the gold pin and the chance to move on to the provincial contest in Red Deer where he might get a write-up in the church magazine or a scholarship to the Bible College.

AN APOLOGY

to the late Stephen Dunning, for not taking the poet William Stafford on a bird-walk in Nichols Arboretum (circa 1987/'88) because I had to go to work in a bookshop.

The timeclock has moved inside
where it holds its ticking sway
more completely than it does
hanging on the wall at work.
It might be called responsibility
if it weren't so silly. I have
to live with what's been done;
they—the tax collectors, money
grubbers, guardians of the ordinary—
have given me a merchant's soul.
When you called to ask if I
would walk through the arboretum
with the old poet, famous
in our small poetry world,
the one we might call "teacher"
if "master" feels too heavy
for our common American ear,
I didn't hesitate. I said
no, of course, the only answer
I've learned. I have to work.
I never thought. The leaves
had finished changing, I imagine,
and most of them were down.
It was nice of you to call.
The walk would have been
remembered by no one but me.

Yet I like to think that maybe
I have a regional knowledge
of trees, geology, bird migrations,
information he might use to make
another beautiful poem, one
that might give some poor soul
(circumscribed by a stupid job
or another hidden timeclock)
pause, and a momentary sense
of the utter loveliness of things.
But that is too much ambition.
I am a clerk. I never met
the poet. I never will.
I went to work, punched in,
did my duty on the register,
and helped a few people buy
things they don't really need.
Outside you walked through the leaves.

FOR THE KIDS WHO YELLED, "HEY, BALDY"

after Thomas Lynch

Remember, children, your own aging
and bring back to youth-sodden minds
this moment when your knees start
their small explosions and your backs
carry the ache of your dull futures.

Remember, O frail youth, Elisha,
tonsured and holy, who called down
two she-bears from the hills
to maul the boys who mocked his baldness.

Remember Elisha and look to the hills
because this prophet on lunch break
calls down bears, hemorrhoids,
bunions, varicose veins, corns,
impotence, and masses of gray hair
to thin the smugness of all your curls.

THROUGH A CRACK IN THE WORLD

I was a grand experiment. They had created everything—trees, bodies, stars, water, time—just to see how I would react. Nothing was as it appeared. They had spent generations trying to convince me that it was real. I was a good subject; usually I believed in their creation. Their children—or their equivalent for children, if they have youth, which is doubtful—spent weeks—which, of course, they don't have either—inventing the names for things. Street, Atlantic, sister, thrush, Seattle. I lapped them up. Originally they intended to take me out of the definitions they had given me and bring me back to reality. But they were too successful. Finally, they realized that if I left the experiment I would crumble, disappear. So they are stuck with me. They have to watch even though they all lost interest long ago. And I have to keep going, worrying about God and the fall of the Roman Empire as if it all matters. A couple of times—in an inexplicable hesitation when my mother turned from a mirror or in an inconsistency behind the eyes of a stranger on a city street far from what I think of as home—I have seen through a crack in the world to the laboratory wall, white and gleaming, with windows. Behind them move indistinct creatures without faces or names.

BEAR STORIES

1.

    Stanley Stewart's aunt read about it in the Calgary paper. A tourist from the States wanted to take his daughter's picture with the black bears at Banff. He coated her hands with honey. He stepped back, the child reached toward the bear like her father told her to do, and he snapped a picture of a bear eating his daughter's hands.

2.

    Never run from a grizzly, old John told me. They'll beat you every time. You can try to climb a tree, but any tree you can climb, a grizzly can too. He'll just walk up it like a ladder. No. The best thing to do is just stand there, and try to get up a big gob of spit in your mouth. Just before a grizzly gets you, he'll stand on his back legs and roar. This is your only chance. When he roars, take that gob of spit and spit it right into his mouth. If you get it back against his throat, he'll turn around and take off. It works better if you're chewing tobacco.

3.

    LaVerne told how his first grizzly charged after the first shot. Since a grizzly's eyes are bad, LaVerne figured she was going for the smell of gunpowder. She came a hundred yards straight for him, LaVerne shooting the whole time. The bear dropped ten feet from his blind. When he gutted her, he found five of his bullets in her heart.

4.

    John and I came back to the main camp after a few days cutting horse trail and found our cook tent ripped to ribbons, the table torn apart, even the stove knocked on its side. A few minutes later I saw the outline of a black bear sitting in the bush at the edge of our clearing.

He must have been accustomed to people, maybe to dumps at mining camps or to other hunting outfits. John gave me the rifle, a small bore goat gun but the only one we had at the time.

"Your first bear," he said.

I tried to aim behind the front leg. I squeezed off the shot slowly, like I'd been told. And the bear howled like a baby, or maybe more like a rabbit that has just been snatched by an owl. He took off through the woods, breaking branches and tearing up bushes. We waited a few hours, hoping the wound would stiffen him up, then followed the blood spots through the forest. About half a mile from camp we found where he had holed up, the ferns pressed down and covered in blood, but the bear was gone. The blood trail gave out soon after.

5.

It was a Sunday. I took my lunch and binoculars, but no gun. I followed a stream up the mountain behind camp until I reached the spring that fed it. Then I crossed a couple of ridges and moved up through the last scrub firs at the tree line. I kept climbing. The only things growing up there were small mountain blueberries. They were ripe and close to the ground. I knelt down and ate them, picking each berry carefully and wiping off the dust of the mountain. I continued climbing until I reached the last high ridge. I sat there, ate my lunch and looked out over the hills and forest below me. I knew our camp was somewhere down there on the edge of the lake, but I couldn't see it. The lake went off to the east for many miles. I could just make out the small valley where it emptied and where the Yukon River started. I pulled my hat over my eyes, lay back in the blueberries, and slept.

As soon as I woke up, I sensed I was not alone and might be in trouble. I raised my hat, then my head, slowly. Below me, back down the mountain maybe a hundred yards but well up from the tree line, a lone grizzly was working his way across the mountain. The fur on his hump caught the sun and seemed almost golden. He looked larger than any animal I had ever seen, bigger than a moose, much stronger than the workhorses on my grandfather's farm. He was raking his claws through the blueberries, pulling out large clumps of them—roots, leaves, dirt—and stuffing everything into his mouth. I could see his teeth even without binoculars. The breeze was blowing up the mountain from the lake, but I still tried not to breathe. The bear didn't turn, didn't look up, just berried his way below me for half an hour. After he had disappeared around a far ridge, I lay, half afraid and without moving, at least an hour longer.

CASHIER'S DREAM; THE HUNT

At that moment, call it the float
if you like, but the precise moment
between your giving me the money
and my giving you the merchandise,
the thing you want or need,
for a small profit—a fair profit,
no one's getting rich here,
just enough to buy food or pay
for my children's clothes or the gas bill—
at that moment we have entered

the hunt, the clear air
of early morning—I have not
moved in an hour or more,
not even swallowed in fear
of frightening off the prey . . .
at that moment I launch
my spear or stone with prayers
that it bring down the brother—
my brother, my prey, you—

and before the bloodletting,
the skinning, I thank the gods
of the hunt, the spirit
of the beast, and I thank you
when you tuck whatever thing
I've sold you under your arm
and begin to leave, returning
to your careless ordinary day.

BOOKSELLER

I don't really care about the characters in books, certainly not about the people who write them. I'm not much interested in their contents, how one book supports or argues with another. I like the objects, the shape and color of them, and the pleasure they take in themselves.

They create abstract patterns: a large red book separated from a small blue one by a used yellow; or a whole shelf assuming twenty shades of green, the variations blending into each other until individual volumes almost disappear. The books make an ever-evolving kaleidoscope, colors shifting into new patterns almost every day.

I prefer to think that it's willed, chosen by the books themselves.

But there is a deeper joy in the bookshop, one that comes despite or because of my need to keep the books in some kind of order. A book on tantric meditation will suddenly appear in the psychology section. I reshelve it. A month later it pops up in the European history section. Six months after it's in the last shelf of the poetry books, looking comfortable between Yeats and Zukofsky. The books find their own order. Their movement seems a dance with a geologic tempo, so slow I can't see it. The dance is like the story country children tell about trees moving at night, just a millimeter or two, nothing that can be noticed in the morning, until one day a child climbs onto a rope swing that's tied to a maple branch, and he swings out as he has done hundreds of times before, but this time slams straight into the side of the barn.

THE 8:35 BUS

Our mornings won't always be like this.
Soon we'll find a little place to rent
out west of town, plant an acre garden
and stay home to fight invading aphids.
We'll build a cabin up north, where snow will keep
us in for weeks, feed evening grosbeaks
and learn the proper way to bank a fire
in our Peacock stove. We'll sail the North Atlantic
from Newfoundland to the Hebrides,
then tan slowly on beaches next to bodies
that will never know one day of work.
We'll measure the semicircle a falcon makes
migrating past our castle in Spain. We will
eat the golden peaches in Samarkand!

LIVY, ABRIDGED

Once I put the baby in her playpen
below our picture window and give her
the green alligator puppet to play
with, I can settle back for a minute
to read about Romulus organizing
shepherds into his city on the hills.
But she starts laughing loudly, and somewhere
between the rape of the Sabine women
and the Tarquinian machinations
to recapture the crown of Rome, I look
over to see her swaying, tentative
on her hands and knees, beginning the first
shuffle across the whole width of her pen.

THEY'RE OUT THERE, WAITING

The man from the Humane Society said
don't trap skunks in June or July.
Babies, he said. Two to ten in a brood.
If you get the mother, the young stay
below and start stinking. Be patient.
Maybe she'll move if you make life hard—
so we stuck mothballs down the hole
and ammonia soaked rags, left
the backyard spotlight on all night,
and played rock 'n' roll on a portable
all day in the shed above her den.
Nothing worked. Finally we let her stay
under the floor where she built her home
just after the garden started to bloom.
We let her take the lily of the valley
and our Siberian iris. We gave her space
and let her be. But now her smell
rises at 3 a.m. We close
our windows and sweat till dawn.
Our shed stinks of musk, and we're afraid
to walk in the yard after dark. We stand
at the kitchen window and look out past
evening primrose and daylilies, wait
for rustling by the compost or ten sets
of stripes hurrying off to the empty lot
out back. But we don't see them. They know
their competition and have learned the rules.
Their paths crisscross our flower beds,

stems and leaves shredded. The edge moves in,
and their smell rises everywhere like
nothing but the clear, sour odor of skunk.

from "CONDITIONS"

If the world becomes so bright
            we can't see the stars,
will they become stories
                       like mythical wars
                               or old gods?
        Or will we—
                    all of us,
       the whole world—
             plan festivals—
say, six hours long,
       on the sixth new moon
of each bright year—
             when we turn off
       all our lights—
             every single bulb—
and dance quietly
       beneath temporary stars?

from "CONDITIONS"

If I had the tongues
of angels,
      what would I say?
I do this, I do that?
           Here's my family?
Here's my house?
      Here's how I get my living?
Occasionally days come when
          there's nothing better
in this expanding universe
      than cherry cobbler?

HITCHHIKING

1.

I don't do it
anymore. I
hope my daughter
never does it.
It's dangerous.
I know. I've read
all about it
in the papers.

But there was once
upon a time,
between 16
and 25,
when I had no
money, a world
to see, and I'd
stick my thumb out
on any road
anywhere and
take off, sooner
or later, to
parts unknown
and to places
where I would find
nothing but fun.

2.

Moose Jaw

I stood beside
the bypass past
Moose Jaw one June
day and night for
19 good hours
and 19 cars
passed me. None stopped.
I played games with
myself (OK
company out
there):

      If a car
doesn't stop in
the next hour, I'll
bury a dime.

And I did it!

If I'm still here
in two hours, I'll
tie my shoelace.

And I did it!

3.

Whitehorse

Hours from the bush,
my left foot wrapped
in bandages,
softly throbbing
from an ax wound,
I sat on my
battered suitcase
filled with dirty
socks, underwear
and too many
books, the Al-Can
Highway sending
up its dust all
over me.

                Fifteen
hundred miles to
Edmonton, then
2000 more
to Chicago.

Sure, I could do
it in a week.

I waited hours
but no long haul
truck driver stopped,
no camper, no

forestry man.
I limped back to
the bus station,
spent half my funds
for an easy
ticket heading
somewhere down south.

4.

Chateauroux

It was Sunday.
I remember
that, but I did
not see a red
castle or stream
or anything
else of interest.
The sun was out,
and I began
to feel warmer,
the Provençal
touch, even though
I wasn't half-
way to the sea.
I didn't speak
one single word
of the language,
had a couple
of friends down in

Toulouse who thought
I might show up
sometime although
they weren't certain.
I was lonely,
of course, but I
was as happy
then, for ten short
minutes, as I've
ever been, beside
a highway, south
bound, my thumb out,
broke, no one to
love anywhere
close, and nothing
to do, no one
to disappoint.

5.

Mt. Pleasant to Mishawaka

It was my last
trip, a straight shot
200 miles
south in July.
I had a chance
to see John, who
had moved west years
before, married,
calmed down, cleaned up,

started a small
company that
fixed foreign cars.
It should have been
easy, a lark.

I hadn't figured
on Grand Rapids,
a city that's
always bigger
than you might think.
I was stranded
for hours downtown,
on an exit
ramp off US
131.
I didn't cross the
Indiana
line till midnight,
saw John and his
wife for 2 hours
before they headed
back west.

       A loss . . .
But they divorced
6 months later.
And I never
again found the
gumption to hitch.

6.

What I've Become

On the first night
of snow, I drive
past a person
standing beside
the freeway, hunched
over against
the wind, one thumb
stuck out. His car
broke down; he is
wearing a suit
and tie, a long
fashionable
black coat. The fear
of hitchhiking
has moved in so
deep I don't stop.
I don't even
think about it.

OLD SONGS AT GREEN LAKE

for Eric and Ann

Between the long peninsula built
its length and breadth with cinderblock
summer homes and the National Music
Camp across the way, loon song—softly
at first, almost unnoticed while we make
our dinner on a grill and walk the dog,
a song like children laughing on a boat
that's drifting off—rises from the lake.

The loons, too, have settled for less
than the ideal; true northern lakes
keep moving north. The loons nest
in reedy corners protected from the wake
of speedboats, do the necessary things
to raise their young, and then, they sing.

THE GUEST CABIN AT ISLE ROYALE

for EK

I'm here, looking out the front window of the cabin they've provided for me. Tobin Harbor. Isle Royale. Lake Superior. The only sound other than birdcall and the occasional outboard is the high ringing of my own blood in my ears. A family of mergansers has been playing in the calm water of the passage between the window and the little island 50 or 60 yards off-shore. A loon floats through but doesn't sing. A black duck dabbles past, its bill almost phosphorescent, greenish yellow. Two spotted sandpipers fly by. Chipping sparrows are nesting in the spruce not 15 feet from the front door of this place. A late wild iris has bloomed in the four hours since I arrived. Two hours ago it was still wrapped around itself.

~

Blue burns in a blue world.
Wild iris—the blue flag—
uncurled in a basalt crack
below spruce and beard moss.
A greeting, if we want it,
from the woman, long dead,
who built her place where
the wail and tremolo
of loon song collect
like the vespers chants
of monks moving to prayer.

The sun at evening prisms
through their windows dappling
the altar red and blue.

CANOEING AGAINST THE WIND

I don't have to do this

two strokes to move a yard

then a breath   a breeze   pushed
back and sideways against rocks

two strokes to move a yard

and my hat blows away

two strokes to move a yard

if this canoe were keeled
it wouldn't catch the wind
blowing from the big lake
up the inlet   pushing

two strokes to move a yard

I'm here because I want
to be   out in the wind

two strokes to move a yard

UPSTREAM ON THE SEICHE

Carried upstream on the seiche—
water pushed back toward its source—
until the flow returns and my canoe
stalls on mud banks. Alder thickets,
mosquitoes, and deer flies. Robins laugh
from the shade. I can do nothing
but slog back, pulling my boat
through slime, slapping at bugs.

Then, high in the mud . . . tracks.

I climb up, kneel before them
and sketch one in my notebook
to compare with a guide at home:
two and three-quarters wide;
three and three-quarters long;
angular toes, the center two
noticeably larger than the two outside.
The track of a small wolf,
its outline clear, the edges sharp,

until the seiche returns and fills
the creek, releasing my canoe.
Water rises to wolf print,
dissolving it, dirt stirred up
then back toward the big lake,
a gentle pull but strong enough
to carry me out past mud banks,
the sedge and rushes, jewelweed

glowing orange, oxeye daisies,
out past the thickets, shaded
at midday, creatures hiding inside.

DREAM OF THE BLACK WOLF

A quick glimpse

                      in my eye's
                      corner

black wolf

        running

                      always running

        ears back
        fur

                      shaggy
                      hackles up
                      a touch

                                  of white
                                  or silver

on its belly

beside the lake
over rock
and lost

        between spruce
        and cedar

        before
I turn

LAMENT FOR THE CRESTED SHELDUCK

(Tadorna cristata)

They're gone now. The last record of them is from North Korea, March, 1971. Two males and four females were swimming in the sea at the mouth of the River Pouchon. Unmistakable. The males: glossy green, almost black on their heads, along the crests that were like manes on their necks; glossy green on their breasts; necks and cheeks paler, gray. The females: white necks; distinctive black and white masks. The bills and legs of both, a brilliant red.

They bred on the quiet patches of rivers in the moist forests of northeast China, North Korea, and a small section of Siberia. They probably wintered along the coasts. Only three specimen skins exist, all in Korean museums. No seasonal variation or juvenile plumage is noted in the books. Their call—if they had one, and they must have had one—was never recorded.

Chekhov may have heard them when he floated east down the Amur in the spring of 1890 on his way to Sakhalin, the prison island. In his long letters to his sister, Masha, or to his editor, Suvorin, he described the thousands of ducks and geese, flying and calling and scurrying from the Russian side of the Amur to the Chinese. The crested shelduck may have been there, and Chekhov might have recognized it from an oriental screen he had seen at the Countess B.'s country estate south of Petersburg. He didn't mention it. The birds would have been part of the mist in the evening, swimming off from the riverboat, reclusive and wary of men.

ON THE EASY LIFE OF SAINTS

after the painting "Saint John the Evangelist on Patmos"
by Joos van Cleve

All of us could choose sainthood,
get rid of ordinary
distractions—bringing the sheep
back home or washing clothes,
spreading manure on the fields
or catching fish, adding what
we can to the everyday
exchange. Sainthood does have its
compensations after all.

Imagine getting locked up
on Patmos, for Christ's good sake,
with a couple of old books,
some blank paper, a new pen,
a distant view of the sea,
time to sit so quietly
that the birds might mistake us
for bushes—then we could all
resolve ultimate questions,
or at least catch a glimpse
of something absolutely
wonderful floating in clouds
of glory.

　　　Then imagine
getting a job—a good job,

not overly demanding,
a job where we could be sure
we weren't harming anyone—
a house, raising a couple
of kids to reasonable
adulthood, and imagine
the slim chance of Vision then.

We're too busy to be saints.
But if the testimony
of the ages and few
intimations in almost
all our lives add up, then we
can hold out for our little
moments of some unearned joy
(while walking dogs, putting the kids
to bed, watching snow fall, when
we get a couple of hours—
unexpectedly—to read).

Maybe that's enough. It's not
Saint John the Evangelist
on Patmos blessed with his sight
of a woman clothed in sea
colors holding a perfect
child, but it's worth something—
our ordinary vision—
and we're almost sure it's real.

MY EDUCATION IN PARIS

An Icelandic woman named Agusta said she wouldn't sleep with me because I was too short.

I had never asked.

A Greek woman, blonder than Agusta, said she wouldn't sleep with me because I was too thin.

I had wanted to ask her, but was too shy.

A young Persian woman, whose name meant "little white flower that grows in the desert"—at least that's what she told me and I wanted to believe her—said she wouldn't sleep with me because I was too old.

I was 22, and I hadn't asked her, either.

A French woman I did ask said she was very pleased but she preferred women.

DAYS OF 1971, 1972

Between my nights washing dishes at the restaurant—
one star in the *Michelin*—where rich folks from Toulouse
ate their quiet country dinners, and my afternoons
on the ledge below the eaves outside my little room
above the private riding club, the ledge that looked south
across green hills to the Pyrenees and where I sat
for eight months and read the expected Europeans—
Celine, of course, Baudelaire, Cavafy in the small prose
fragments of his French translation—and for the first time
understood what it was about the Americans—Poe,
Melville, Whitman, Henry Miller—how they could be sad
and exuberant on the same page and how right
that sounded to me . . . in the mornings between my job
and the reading, she would come back tired and smelling
of her other, more experienced lovers and would wake
me, sometimes gently caressing my beard or bringing
me back to her hard world by quietly ripping pages
from my books and dropping them on me like a blanket.

BLACK ICE

Some things shouldn't frighten me. I should know better. If given half a chance at a party or over drinks, I will bore my friends with stories about ice skating across prairie sloughs forty years ago, learning how to turn quickly and handle a puck. Yet when my seven-year-old daughter and I drive down by the Huron River after a two-week cold snap and find the large pond behind Barton Dam completely frozen and carrying several families of skaters, I feel the flutter of my new and overeducated fear. Of course I let her go out on the ice. I go with her. We stare down through several inches of black ice at the plants drifting in the slight current. We hope to see a cold fish swim by. She kicks a stone across the ice, squealing with pleasure at its speed and distance. She wants to kick it all the way across, over to the marina below the rich people's homes.

That's when I get scared. I call her back and climb out on the dike above the water. She keeps kicking her stone across the ice, and I notice pressure cracks. I begin to imagine the groans and cracks of ice.

"Come on, Faith. We have to go," I call out, and she ignores me as she has done for most of her life.

I keep calling, and still she ignores me, kicking her rock across the frozen river, sliding on her feet, her knees, even her butt, laughing and laughing. I call again, more urgently, and then again. I try to sound tough and threaten loss of privileges. She kicks the rock out farther and keeps going.

METAPHOR FOR THE LONG MARRIED

Beyond familiarity
there is a small lighted space—
comfortable, bright enough
without blinding, warm enough
for relief on a cold day—
a small place surrounded
by an interesting darkness
where you travel at leisure,
a place that glows at the edge
of perception, that always
waits to take you back inside.

AFTER TWENTY YEARS

for Christine

We sat above the rocks
below Big Sur one spring
morning and watched snowy
egrets dance, their breeding
plumes arching backward
as they raised their yellow feet
hesitantly from the surf
before he mounted her
and egret generations
began their tentative
futures. Our kinship with
snowy egrets was nothing
grand: perhaps we understood
their single-mindedness and hoped
they felt some kind of pleasure
too. It looked as if they did.

AN INTRODUCTION TO MODERN GREEK IN SOUTH BEND, INDIANA, 1967

for Vassilis Lambropoulos
Artemis Leontis
and Kostalena Michelaki

Quince and pomegranate? Sage? Rosemary?
I didn't know anyone who even knew
what those things were, so at Benner's Market
on Mishawaka Avenue, right next
to our new temple—the Gospel Center
United Missionary Church—I bought
pistachio nuts—A Product of Greece—
and Welch's White Grape Juice. I carried them
like holy food to Potawatomi
Park where at picnic tables below oaks
I read *Zorba the Greek.* I was fifteen
and there had never been a loneliness
and a longing as exquisite as mine.
I wandered over dusty hills in Crete
slaking my thirst with Welch's. I sauntered
through dark alleys in the medieval town
on Rhodes—built by the Knights Hospitaler
after Saladin conquered Jerusalem—
and smelled souvlaki grilling over fire,
eating pistachios to satisfy
my hunger. When lake effect snow began
to drift down from the sullen skies above
South Bend, I discovered Odysseus

Elytis and learned that in those poems
was some place new. But I walked there
in the sun on a beach sprinkled with white
and black pebbles, with a slightly older
dark-haired olive-skinned woman who whispered
just above the Aegean's gentle wash:
E thalassa, thalassa, thalassa.

DIRECTIONS TO NORTH FISHTAIL BAY

If you paddle down past
the point where the eagles
hang out, you're almost there.
It's best like this—a hint
of fog flittering across
the lake before a breeze.
No sun, sky gray, but calm,
not a ripple or a wave.
Just round the next point, where
the sand drops away fast
under luminous deep green
water . . . And you made it!
Go now. It looks like rain.

You'll hear a hermit thrush
calling, hidden in the pines
or in a cedar swamp
where, when you look hard
into the dark, you will see
a profusion of iris,
almost purple and fresh
on this day, the very day you've
come alone to North Fishtail Bay.
There's thunder in the west.
Go now. It looks like rain.

THE DAY AFTER AN ICE STORM

When it dawns crystalline, blue,
the air sparkling with prisms
reflected off oak and spruce,
off every twig, branch, or limb,
even off trees cascading
over fences, trees uprooted
by the splendor of ice—
the day lifts us, takes us out-
side ourselves, outside the news
of a nurse driving back home
last night, at the blackest hour
of the ice storm, when I was
watching electrical arcs
illuminating the yard.
I heard trees break apart
and was thrilled with fear. She stopped
to help at an accident—
it looked far worse that it was—
when a young man, twenty-three,
leaving work in his truck,
spun out on the ice killing
the nurse, who, in a brief moment
of faith, might have imagined
today dawning crystalline,
brittle, gloriously cold.

A MONK'S RULE

for Christine

But for you, my love,
I would take a monk's rule.
Rise long before dawn,
have a simple breakfast
of unbuttered toast and milk.
One cup of coffee, black.
I would go upstairs,
sit with paper and pen,
and plumb the deepest reaches
of my mind or soul or self.
Evenings I would read
nothing but books written
in the first millennium.

THE ROAD FROM GALAHAD

The boy who became the preacher who became
my father first saw God in a snowstorm
while he walked, hunched against the weather,
north on the road from Galahad, Alberta.

God-smacked, like Paul, while walking home
for evening chores, he fell to his knees right there
on frozen gravel next to a frozen slough
on a Sunday night. March, 1936.

Soon enough the slough would fill with willets,
marbled godwits, and canvas-back ducks dodging
coyotes and breeding furiously before they flew
their long routes back to Caribbean beaches,

but this night whatever the boy saw in the snow
drifting against fence posts, snow so thick
it lightened the sky, whatever he saw was enough
to sustain him through that century of doubt.

ALL THE TIME YOU WANT

Take the chain from the gate. Walk in.
No one really cares. Most of the stones
have faded, are cracked or broken.

Designed as a churchyard
like the ones left behind
in the Old Country, the yard

outlasted its church. All the kids
who could moved to town years ago.
Someone mows, but not often.

Here you are free to invent
whatever tales you need.
Please, take all the time you want.

See that obelisk, barely a yard tall
tilting over in the back corner,
about to fall—it marks

another common story: early death,
illness, and a miserable marriage.
If you think you have some time,

you can pick weeds from the plot
or try to right that stone.
There's little else to do here.

APOLOGIA

We shrink the palette, some of us anyway,
until things get simple, like those few paintings
by Monet where he dispensed with sunsets
and cathedrals and seemed content doing snow.

Somber, write the curators about mauve, blue,
flat green, and white, as if they've never
breathed cold air, felt it sharp and dry,
lively as a knife deep in their humid lungs.

Ten steps back and canvas becomes photograph;
twenty, and it disappears—but somewhere out there
waits the exultation of the cracking ice,
the shiver and the fear just before a thaw.

A WALK

1.

. . . from that place in a hall in an old farmhouse,
at the foot of a narrow stairway that rose
up to darkness at the top—no one believes
I can remember my first steps; *you heard it
from your family,* they say, but I remember
I was alone and no one saw the things I saw;
I know a man who remembers his own birth,
I say, who remembers pain when he was pushed
into his life—and I pulled myself upright
by that stairway, turned and walked, uncertainly
of course, back to the living room and the light.

2.

. . . on New Year's Eve after I snuck out of church—
the Watch Night Service where my family watched
minutes crawl, sang hymns, and prayed until midnight—
and outside in air so cold it hurt to breathe,
air that rose up dense and smoky around me
when I walked fast, faster over the snow
crunching back at me, until I was running,
exhilarated, until the twelve bells chimed
and the drunk and godless yelled through their windows
to the boy running by—*Happy New Year, kid!*—
and all I wanted was to join the party.

3.

. . . alone from the East Station to the river,
then west through courtyards and the palace gardens—
and somewhere here among the fountains the sun
finally broke through the trees, over the shops
and hotels onto the first old man reading
his morning paper on a bench wet with dew—
to the Fields of Heaven and all the way up
to the Place of the Star—and I understood,
or thought I did for a minute, maybe two,
the notion that the sun might need one of us
each morning (and this morning it might be me)
to bring it back over the crest with the power
of our joy—and I returned to the river
to stand in line before the sparkling tower.

4.

. . . in the Manistee National Forest
on snowshoes, probably four feet on the ground
already and more snow falling, and I lost
direction out in the scrub oak and jack pine,
then wandered for hours hearing only raven
croaks and the deceptively close nuthatch calls,
nasal and metallic, until I stumbled
upon a snowed-under, fire-access, two-track road
I vaguely remembered and found my way back
to my friends, their cabin, their woodstove and fire.

A DEDICATION

for Christine

I might stand on a catwalk
built through a forest canopy
with any stranger. I could stare
into the eye of a cerulean warbler
frantically singing to mark territory
or call in a mate. But if I walk
through a vineyard that slopes
down toward the sea, I will
walk, my love, only with you.

AT THE WENDY'S EAST OF SALINE

for Anne Carson

Behind the back parking lot
close to the factory
that makes molded plastic parts—
bumpers, knobs, and cupholders
for the big Ford pickup trucks—
in a scrubby stand of oaks
next to a subdivision
of vinyl-sided houses,
a great horned owl peers
over the edge of her nest,
seemingly unperturbed,
as if she has been watching there
for two or three thousand years.

MY DAUGHTER'S NARCOLEPSY

Before we received the official
diagnosis, we loved to recount
her sleep episodes. My favorite,
the Louvre, in front of those gigantic
paintings David made celebrating
the coronation of Josephine
and Napoleon before the French
nobles. My daughter drooled on the bench.

EVIDENCE

for Ted Anderson

The evidence of things not seen is
in their song, like whippoorwills calling
from an old field above the river
at the last hint of twilight, pink sky
finally giving up to the dark,
echoing calls rising from bracken,
from birds seen only as quick shadows
whose song might move even the mountains.

THE CRITICISM OF MY FRENCH POEMS

Our relationship was probably
over by then, but I let her read
the only copies—each clean and short
with simple, fragile lines. She walked past
a window, reached out, and dropped them all.
I saw poems fluttering onto streets
or into those clipped Parisian trees.
Some caught a breeze, floating up, away.

THE LAST ROOST

There's a record written years later—
up in Emmet County, after months
of slaughter—50,000 a day
sent to Chicago—the passenger
pigeons rose in their last flock, circled
over Lake Michigan, terrified
of land, and finally exhausted,
rested, relieved perhaps, in water.

CHASING THE ANCIENT MURRELET

Ancient . . . because of a gray mantel
     thrown over its shoulders,
    which look hunched against the weather

of the North Pacific, its real home,
     too far from this place
    at the edge of Lake Michigan

to be imagined, where the untouched
     but beautiful young
    run down the beach in summertime

longing to leave their parents, who make
     steel appliances
    and claim to love the wind and winter.

The bird is lost or brave or blown here
     by westerlies strong
    enough to reshape its instincts,

to bring it down to the dirty mouth
     of a river that drains
    the abandoned car factories

of South Bend, and the ancient murrelet
     bobs in these choppy
    irregular freshwater swells,

diving, often, after crustaceans
                    that haven't lived here
            for a geologic epoch,

but taking what minnows it can find
                    to keep hunger off
            and it dies, here, in a place

it doesn't belong, where it can't find
                    the right food or mate
            but where I find it, following

clear directions on the internet,
                    to catch a quick glimpse—
            as it rises between waves—

of its two-toned bill, and the large head—
                    bulky, oversized
            on its small, diminished body.

WHEN THE GIRLS ARRIVED IN COPENHAGEN

and left the station, near midnight,
snow fell in soft piles on their hats
and backpacks.

No cars or people passed
while they walked
down the hushed streets.

Through windows without blinds or curtains
they could see Danes bathed in blue
television light

or quietly reading in uncluttered rooms
small novels perhaps about two girls
long ago walking through snow.

A NEW LANGUAGE

Once you get past the poison ivy
and cobwebs covering
the door, once you find a way
to push it open—using a crowbar,
then oiling the hinges—

a hall
stretches ahead, clean,
uncluttered, lined
with unopened cabinets.

There's a faint scent
of lily-of-the-valley in the air,
or, perhaps, of lilac.

STATUE OF THE BLIND GIRL

Nydia, the blind flower girl of Pompeii, after
Edward Bulwer-Lytton and Randolph Rogers

She listens, not to the green world exploding
around her, not to Vesuvius howling—

the hour has come; of two working in the field
one shall be taken; of two women grinding wheat
one shall be taken; Vesuvius erupts
and the black clouds descend; now we know
this is the hour when the thief will come—

she listens, not to the temples collapsing
or the birds crying from the shriveled gardens,

she listens for the one voice who must call,
the one who knows, now that the hour has come,
that she can take us to the boats

and she suffers with our trembling earth,
gagging like the rest of us in this closed air,

but when we walk around her,
to the shadowed side, closer to the wall,
we can see the hidden profile,

the one that disguises her joy

now that the hour has come,
the one that shows her smile.

SEA AND RAIN: LAKE MICHIGAN

After James McNeill Whistler, 1865

There is a dance at water's edge,
a movement between the lake, its sand,
and the horizon where lake becomes cloud.

Between those lines our world's
a thin wash of muted tones, beige
and gray with a hint of white,

almost abstract, until the dancer
steps out into the pool.
She makes the whole thing real.

JOHN GLENN HIGH SCHOOL, WESTLAND, MICHIGAN

Homage to Mike Kelley

My first gig as visiting writer—
and they were excited too. Someone
made blue fliers for the doors and windows—
The poet is coming! The poet is
coming! The day I arrived someone
else had tagged every one of them—
in your mouth
in your mouth
in your mouth

SUMMER TEACHING

Driving the young scientists back
from a beaver dam, I listen to their talk

about life as information
encoded in letters
between spiraling strands of protein,
how we will soon
digitize our sequences
and the information that is us,
everything about us,
will never die.

I drive carefully on the back roads
and the freeway, hoping that whatever gods
left today haven't heard
or are off chasing beautiful children
who escape by turning into trees.

STONE TOOLS

After John M. O'Shea

Three thousand years ago someone stopped
on a small hill, unnoticed now
behind a postwar subdivision
but only a block up from the river.

He sat on a large rock, a glacial
erratic, for an afternoon and chipped
a stone point from a piece of chert.

He left his sharp-edged flakes scattered
And glistening under the oak leaves.

I WILL LIFT UP MINE EYES

When the world is finally theirs again,
they will come down from the hills
out west of town.
They'll follow straight lines—
they learn so quickly!—even using the bridges
that haven't yet crumbled
into walls or into nothing at all.

When they stop to hunt rats
or racoons at a house
broken open when oaks blew over,
they'll step gingerly—they are always
so careful where they place their paws—
on what's left of our moldy books,
avoiding the still shimmering plastic
shards of the Anthropocene.

THE FORGER'S EDUCATION

The weight of brush in hand, the length
and pressure of brushstroke – that was my gift,
my genius. That took little study.

In time I learned to live
within my limitation, learned I'd never see

the longing in a quiet room,
the gaze out past the painting
to all the other stories
no one else could ever understand.

AUTHOR'S NOTES

THE COVER PAINTING, *The Dress of the Poem* by Syrian artist Khaled Al-Saa'i, was commissioned by the University of Michigan Museum of Art for its 2022 exhibition *Watershed* , which was curated by Jennifer M. Friess. Al-Saa'i found my poem "Sea and Rain: Lake Michigan," which is included in this collection, translated it into Arabic, then used the words and letters from the translation to create the swirl at the center of his painting. My poem is an ekphrastic reaction to James Abbott McNeil Whistler's *Sea and Rain* (1865) from UMMA's collection.

"An Introduction to Modern Greek"

E thalassa = Η θάλασσα = The sea.
In Greek, this has been the same word since long before Homer, all the way to today's newspaper.

ACKNOWLEDGMENTS

THE AUTHOR IS RESPONSIBLE FOR all copyrighted material.

I may have forgotten where some of these poems first appeared or might have misplaced a record or two or more, and if so, I apologize to the editors. But I think the publication acknowledgment below is mostly accurate.

Some of these poems, sometimes in different forms and under different titles, first appeared in

The Academy of American Poets Poem-a-Day web site, The Alternative Press, *The Bear River Review*, *The Beloit Poetry Journal*, *Big Scream*, *The Bonfire Review*, *Border Crossing*, *Caliban*, *The Collagist*, *Escape Into Life*, *The Fiddlehead*, *The Great Lakes Review*, *The Green River Review*, *Hanging Loose*, *I Stay Home*, *Iowa Review*, *The MacGuffin*, *Michigan Quarterly Review*, *New Ohio Review*, *Notre Dame Review*, *Notus*, *Oleander*, *Pank*, *Parting Gifts*, *Passages North*, *Phoebe*, *Pivot*, *Poor Claudia*, *Red Cedar Review*, *The Southern Review*, *Witness*, *The Wittenberg Review*, and *The Wooster Review*.

"On the Easy Life of Saints," first appeared in the anthology *A Visit to the Gallery*, edited by Richard Tillinghast and published by the University of Michigan Museum of Art.

"All the Time You Want" was commissioned by Evan Chambers for his symphonic song cycle, *The Old Burying Ground*, and was read in performance at Kerrytown Concert House, and with the University of

Michigan Symphony Orchestra at Hill Auditorium, Oberlin College, Cornell University, and Carnegie Hall.

"Apologia" and "At the Wendy's East of Saline" first appeared in the local anthology *Writers Reading at Sweetwater,* edited by Chris Lord.

While looking back at the very early poems, I discovered that four or five of them were included in a thesis I submitted as part of a Master of Arts degree at Central Michigan University in 1982. It had the rather unimaginative title *Themes and Variations.* My gratitude to Eric Torgersen, for insisting that I finish that collection.

Most, but not quite all, of the poems appeared in one and/or another of the following books and chapbooks:

Learning to Dance (Ann Arbor, Mi.: Falling Water Books, 1985).

Weather Report (Roseville, Mi.: Ridgeway Press, 1988).

Dream of the Black Wolf (Roseville, Mi.: Ridgeway Press, 1993).

Detail from the Garden of Delights (Saline, Mi.: Limited Mailing Press, 1993).

Life Science and Other Stories (Brooklyn, NY.: Hanging Loose Press, 1995).

Everything I Need (Greensboro, North Carolina: March Street Press, 1996).

The Huron River: Voices from the Watershed, co-edited with John Knott (Ann Arbor, Mi.: The University of Michigan Press, 2000).

Guilty at the Rapture (Brooklyn, NY: Hanging Loose Press, 2006).

If the World Becomes So Bright (Detroit, Mi.: Wayne State University Press, 2009).

Marginalia for a Natural History (Pittsburg, Pa.: Black Lawrence Press, 2011).

The Ancient Murrelet (Ann Arbor, Mi.: Alice Greene & Co., 2013).

Fidelities (Ann Arbor, Mi.: Alice Greene & Co., 2015).

The Bird-while (Detroit, Mi.: Wayne State University Press, 2017).

Some of these poems were written or revised when I had fellowships from the National Endowment for the Arts and the Michigan Council for the Arts and Cultural Affairs, or when I had residencies at the Detroit YMCA through The Writer's Voice, at Isle Royale National Park (twice), at the International Centre for Writers and Translators of Rhodes, Greece, and at the University of Michigan Biological Station.

I continue to be grateful for the support and encouragement of Steve Gillis.

ABOUT THE AUTHOR

KEITH TAYLOR HAS AUTHORED OR edited 18 books and chapbooks, the most recent of which, published in 2021, is *Let Them Be Left: Isle Royale Poems*. His last full length collection, *The Bird-while*, was published by Wayne State University Press and won the Bronze medal for the Foreword/Indies Poetry Book of the Year. He has received Fellowships from the National Endowment for the Arts and the Michigan Council for the Arts and Cultural Affairs, among others. After a series of mostly menial but formative jobs, he worked for most of twenty years as a bookseller, before teaching for a few years in the writing programs at the University of Michigan.